Second Wind

Second Wind

David Graham

Texas Tech University Press
1990

This book was set in 10 on 13 Clearface and printed on acid-free paper that meets the guidelines for permanence and durability of the Committee on Production Guidelines for Book Longevity of the Council on Library Resources.⊗

Jacket and book design by Joanna Hill
Cover art by Lee Shippey

Printed in the United States of America

Library of Congress Cataloging-in-Publication Data
Graham, David, 1953–
    Second wind / David Graham.
      p. cm.
     ISBN 0-89672-210-4 (alk. paper). — ISBN 0-89672-211-2 (pbk. :
alk. paper)
     I. Title
    PS3557.R193S4   1990
    811'.54—dc20   89-20388
                                                    CIP

For Lee

As our blood labors to beget
    Spirits, as like souls it can,
Because such fingers need to knit
    That subtle knot, which makes us man:
So must pure lovers' souls descend
    To affections, and to faculties,
Which sense may reach and apprehend,
    Else a great prince in prison lies.

—Donne, "The Ecstasy"

Foreword

Intelligent, hardwon, and immensely readable, *Second Wind* numbers among the finest poetry books of recent years. In the broadest sense, David Graham's theme is nothing less than mortality: how we live, die, and affect each other along the way. The book is also a beautifully complex anthem of America in its variety, as it was and is. These poems helped me to a fresh understanding of the small towns one drives through on the way to grander destinations, the posturing of adolescent boys growing up to be "men / foolish as boys but stronger," the accuracies and deceptions of our language. Although the poems' subjects are often local and familiar, their achieved ambitions are never small: a reference to Hiroshima, for instance, widens the sweep and reach of family history in "A Sense of Scale." The informing intelligence is original and mature: this is the work of a grown-up, wise beyond our years. Graham is acquainted with the chance at the heart of the atom. He faces the possibility that events spring from entropy rather than a divine order, that the past is "all twinkling sky / of hit and near miss, the same stars / wheeling, giving shapelessness its shape." Yet he also celebrates a world in which people carry on, despite this knowledge, "nodding / and smiling, all out of hope / and decent proportion." What's more, the book is so beautifully written that you won't want to put it down. I seldom see language move with such grace; there are sentences one wants to reread for the sinuous music of their construction. Lately it's fashionable to say that the most compelling poetry is coming from Eastern Europe, or England, or Anywhere-But-Here. And there are those who feel that all the poetry worth reading has already been written. David Graham's *Second Wind* is a vigorous argument against such cranky notions. It succeeds in doing that difficult thing: giving pleasure as it makes us think.

Alice Fulton

Acknowledgments

Thanks to the editors of the following journals and anthologies, where many of these poems have appeared, sometimes in earlier versions:

Anthology of Magazine Verse and Yearbook of American Poetry, 1986–87: Rough Air
Antietam Review: "Self-Portrait with Australia"
Artemis: "What It Is Like"
Blueline: "The Mohawk River: A Real Allegory of Twenty Years of My Life as an Artist"
Caliban: "Self-Portrait as Author and Citizen"
Cutbank: "The Valley Where We Live"
Hawaii Review: "Boys and Fireworks"
Oxford Magazine: "Why I Love Halloween"
Painted Bride Quarterly: "Breaking and Entering"
Ploughshares: "Planxty Beethoven"; "Rough Air"
Poetry: "The Day I Cannot Stop Crying"; "Kinds of Jazz"; "The Mind's Eye"; "Self-Portrait with Self-Doubt"; "Self-Portrait with Stage Fright"; "Self-Portrait with Nostalgia"
Prairie Schooner: "The Fox, a Most Cat-like Dog"; "Self-Portrait as Lucky Man"; "Wedding Gift"
Sweet Nothings: An Anthology of Rock and Roll in American Poetry: "Father of the Man"; "Jesus Never Sleeps"
Wisconsin Review: "Farewell to Music: Turlough O'Carolan (1670–1738)"; "First Snow, Wisconsin"
Worcester Review: "Unguided Tour of Floyd, Virginia"; "Guided Tour of Pocahontas, Virginia"; "Near Misses"

The poems in Part I, Common Waters, were published originally as a chapbook, by Flume Press (1986).

For years of valuable criticism and invaluable friendship, particular thanks to Dennis Finnell and Joe Donahue.

 Contents

PART I
Self-Portrait with Nostalgia   3
Like a Television   5
The Mohawk River: A Real Allegory of Twenty Years of
   My Life as an Artist   7
Boys on Schedule   8
Self-Portrait from D to G   11
Mother Pills   12
A Sense of Scale   13
Self-Portrait with Self-Doubt   15
Breaking and Entering   16
Companion of Dusk   17
Boys and Fireworks   18
Boy Gone Haywire   20
Boys Backward and Forward   22
The Attic Which Is Not Desire   23
Common Waters   24

PART II
Self-Portrait with Stage Fright   31
Self-Portrait with Australia   32
The Day I Cannot Stop Crying   33
Unguided Tour of Floyd, Virginia   35
Guided Tour of Pocahontas, Virginia   37
Near Misses   39
The Mind's Eye   41
Loons   42
Wedding Gift   45
Father of the Man   46
The Valley Where We Live   47
Why I Love Halloween   48
Self-Portrait as Author and Citizen   50

PART III
Letter from London   53
Kinds of Jazz   55
Planxty Beethoven   56
Farewell to Music: Turlough O'Carolan (1670–1738)   57
Planxty Beatles   59

Planxty Charles Ives   60
Planxty Lee Morgan   61

PART IV
Sure   65
Rough Air   66
Moon Walk   67
Jesus Never Sleeps   68
The Fox, a Most Cat-like Dog   70
Self-Portrait as Lucky Man   71
What It Is Like   72
Hickory Fall   73
First Snow, Wisconsin   74
Second Wind   75
Dust Events   77

Part I

Self-Portrait with Nostalgia

A town without delicatessens,
without tenements and subways,
without a bookstore or movie theater—
my town has all these things on TV,
so I grow happy as an islander
on a National Geographic special,
enjoying my electric mixer
before there is electricity.
How to tell the blind from the blind?
Back in these days every boy
has basement guitar and amplifier
rehearsing a single song: out of here,
out of here, out of here.
I am the world's littlest brother,
coming with my new Louisville Slugger
to the vacant lot where my brother
will make them let me play.
And I am magic: pick a card,
and I know which one before you do,
though if you refuse my game
I will also know why better than anyone.
My thoughts that do often lie too deep for tears
are of cherry bombs, elaborate jackknives,
the sudden breasts of the neighbor girl
beginning to wallpaper my dreams.
Not only have I never heard of Martin Luther,
Albrecht Durer, Vergil, or Neville Chamberlain,
my town has few Jews, no Blacks or Puerto Ricans,
just several different brands of Catholic
making their stand along the shallow, polluted creek
that divides our town from itself.
The mayor runs things from the office

of his Dodge dealership, with its girly calendar
and patriotic ashtrays.

            Every night
I search for the strategic satellites
that will be spying on all this:
feathers in a sparrow's moulting tail,
heat rising from illicit beds,
the subversive sighs that escape me
like air from crushed pillows,
even the smell of milk in our refrigerator
as, unknown to all, it goes bad at midnight.
But all I see are fireflies, drifting planets,
beacons from the new shopping plaza,
and the landing lights of prop jets
lowering for the approach to larger towns.

Like a Television

Like a dim view through this window
or music half remembered from
a vacant unlit theater,
or the voice on my telephone
of a friend not far from crying,
like a clock without face I sing,
ungodly muse, in whom I do
not trust, my penny-ante love,
I sing the unsteady visions
of childhood, names of my schoolmates
and friends rolling like film credits
at night beneath my eyelids. So
I sing my not-proud confession
of a boy I locked in a cellar
when we were five, of the thick lies
I told to keep him there and slip
the blame, while police cars cruised,
teachers searched the playground, and parents
were phoned. But he never tattled
when he was found, never blamed me—
and wanted instead to be friends.
Still, I'd hurt him because he was
one of those boys everyone hurts,
so of course I snubbed him, just as
if he'd been cruel to me—as
in a way he had. Years later
when he was thrown from a fast car
and finally beaten to death
by the weight of that hapless body,
I read the newspaper report
feeling the momentary flush
of guilt and thrill that we call shock.
Therefore I sing, though I should talk,
of Jeffrey Olsen, rest in peace,
for whom I have no right to sing
and whose real name I can't recall.
One more declarative sentence

with little to declare, I'll sing,
with my dream voice stammering "here,"
like a television whose sound
has conquered its wavering sight,
like nothing at all but myself.

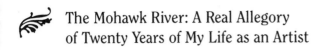 The Mohawk River: A Real Allegory
of Twenty Years of My Life as an Artist

Where I came from the slow river unrolled
placid as a bridle path, between fields
dotted with grazing Holsteins. I came slow
down unlined roads, my bicycle pursued
by dogs driven crazy with solitude.
With carseats propped on porches neighbors sat
to note my going, and whistle their dogs back
soon enough. Too slow to know better
I often dismounted at this farmhouse
and that, quiet and awkward during grace
and the food they made me try. I had time
for anything, and therefore did little
but tell stories embellished from those days
I was escaping. The river got even
duller for the telling. Barges appeared,
slow and steady as garbage trucks. I made
my town smaller, took away its paper
and movies, adding just some luncheonettes
where waitresses called me by name. In time
I remembered horse-drawn delivery trucks,
two-digit phone numbers, and a few men
damaged for good on the courthouse benches.
Where did I get such a town? Is it true,
each morning the radio announcer
read the names of boys and girls with birthdays,
and did the crossword puzzle on the air?
That firemen actually rescued kittens
from trees? I remember each of these things
and don't much care if they're true. Slow river
of anyone's past, meandering names
of any local faith—I return now
more to praise than to remember. The tribe
from whom my river gained its name—Mohawk—
is nearly gone. Their name means man-eater.

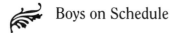 Boys on Schedule

It was junior high
(even the name murmuring "in-between")
I first saw the oncoming days
aimed at my childhood.
Earlier hints didn't matter—
a cat with cracked skull
twitching in the street
at the hub of a bloody puddle,
or the friend I tossed, with
my one judo move, to the sidewalk—
who lay there a second too long.
My first deep glimpse at the book
no one willingly reads
came on schedule in eighth grade
when, however it was for girls,
for a boy honor flared
in every slap and jimmied locker,
every secret scratched on a bathroom wall.
Those who were afraid weren't afraid
to egg others on, and he
who refused a fight knew
the permanent penalty.
And so came our first match
that wasn't just wary shoving
and maybe a quick tussle
on the grass. Two bigmouths
(whose dispute has long faded
into old math scores and locker
combinations), after sparring
all day in corridors, being
cornered by a crowd of boys,
finally named a place and time—
after school, just off the grounds
on a wide lawn sheltered
with maples (where we'd meet
for a pre-school cigarette).
At the last bell they strolled

straight from homeroom to street,
trailing their comet's tails
of eager seconds. My favorite
was Bobby, friend since kindergarten,
tall, blonde, beginning to show
the muscles of a man. He was
in my church school class,
a fellow acolyte, and, in truth,
smarter than he pretended to be—
a bad bet, as I didn't know then,
to win without rules. Steve was smaller,
quick tempered, delinquent, mean—
he wore cowboy boots and tight black jeans
and already a tattoo on one wrist.
There were no rules, and thus no hope
for Bobby, who despite size and strength
lived as I did in the world
of breakaway chairs, justice,
pantomime punches from which a man
climbed to win. Steve played cat-and-mouse
a while, then, after trading
timid feints and jabs, let Bobby
lean into his first real punch,
and though Bobby kept
his feet, you could see his loss
blooming, his face never again
so baby-pink as when
that purple welt on his cheekbone
began to rise. Maybe a dozen
more slugs closed one eye
and bloodied his nose and lips—
still he kept his balance, propped
by our chants tapering to jeers.
He may have gotten a few hits in
but they were nothing
but the forlorn twitchings of pride.
At the arrival of the screeching
Polish neighbor, he looked so glad

our taunts turned wooden.
She dispersed us with upraised broom
and a tirade on Communism.
"You're bad as Russians," she cried,
"fighting in streets." Even then
I knew she was wrong—
communists don't fight on the street,
boys do, and then men
foolish as boys but stronger.

Self-Portrait from D to G

A short hop of the alphabet, two blocks
I fingered for hours when I was a boy,
from D to G with a strange "if" between,
from dross to gold I could almost believe
in the alchemy of a transformed self,
but for the toneless song my mother sang
over the rooftops of my childish world,
and sings again over the telephone.

The two-note song she made of my first name
was my pocketwatch that would never quit
until I heard the syllable and a half
of my last name in the November wind.
I'm still waiting, having pulled off the face
to reveal the flywheel thick with dust,
the stem bent beyond further winding—
the works look gutted, yet still rouse each night
for a few steady revolutions.
As any child is a damaged garden
so am I. Perhaps this drama is good
so long as dead weeds grow again. Perhaps
I'd like newspaper headlines of my name
in flames above distant roofs and hillsides—
the loyal dog who walked through inferno
to save a girl and be damaged for good.
From dread to grace, it's a short wait, I thought,
from dog to strange god as from dross to gold,
in a terrible dream of full gladness.

 Mother Pills

Who couldn't sleep? A boy with diseases
lifted from *Readers' Digest,* a new one
each month: tuberculosis, leukemia,
fear of open places, dread of the new.

I pestered my mother, who brought me pills
in the night, aspirin she called magic,
the very narcotic I pleaded for.
Some nights they were, and I drifted away.

Who cannot sleep? A man married to fear,
mothered now by long distance, each new list
of her ailments I tend and count like sheep.
Her comforting voice still rains on my roof.

Surely she cannot forget being kicked
from within, my pink-footed scrabbling
for release. That's why she takes each misstep
as aimed at her. That's why she swallows pills

to heal me of her memory. That's why
my fitful rolling in bed can wake her.
Yet regardless of my insomnia
her crippled hip will act up tonight.

In the years since I called her in the dark,
habits die hard. Visiting her these days,
I hear the all-hours radio complaining,
her murmurs to my father in a new voice.

I think of my gradeschool essay on her:
how much she loved horses, how she was tall,
how every night as she stood at the stove
she retold us what a bad cook she was.

I may also have drawn her long hair, eyes split
behind bifocal lenses, but what remains
is that sliver of light under my bedroom door,
the voice my voice could waken, sure as rain.

A Sense of Scale

We played pig-face, my brother and I,
for soldiers on convoy down the Thruway,

whole truckfuls of baggy green men
fresh from high school, boots black as showroom tires.

Dad found it easy to pass a Jeep
in no hurry, so we mugged "Anchors Aweigh"

to see if those Army men would notice.
"Pipe down," called Dad, but then

Mom whistled "Bridge On The River Kwai,"
calling it by some other name,

and sang all the verses in a brassy voice
we'd never heard before. She was a sergeant

in the War, we told all our friends,
and Dad just a corporal—though he got

to fly to the Philippines while she typed memos
in Enid, Oklahoma. In browning snapshots

they ambled hand in hand on pass or furlough
until their olive drab marriage spliced

with someone's reconnaissance shots and tourist views:
calendar vista of Mt. Fuji through the trees;

a whorehouse in Manila maybe,
where dark-skinned women without shirts

lounged among Dadless soldiers in smoky rooms;
one withered Filipino peasant with breasts sagging

to her waist—captioned "Old Saddlebags"
in a hand not my father's;

what we called "a jap" incinerated grinning
halfway out of a tank turret; another,

driftwood bones and scraps of flesh
sunk into sand on an unlabelled beach.

Stranger still, Dad himself, in a jungle
with a dozen buddies, stripped down

for volleyball or swimming, smiling at the future.
"It wasn't bad for us," he would say,

"we needed lights and running water
for the darkroom. We could cool down."

Still, he was so skinny and frail
we hooted all the louder at this Thruway's

crop of aimless privates, with their plugs and gum,
their sunday-driving nonchalance.

At the rest area, Dad and Mom got carried away
saluting each empty Jeep in the parking lot.

I did not think then of the final shots
in that album they never mentioned

but allowed us to find in our nosings—
aerial views, but low, of Hiroshima

not long after the blast. Acres of rubble,
just like our town dump, but with here and there

a chimney, phone pole, or charred tree trunk
to give us a sense of scale.

Self-Portrait with Self-Doubt

At the playground as a boy I saw myself
in those kids teachers called "special," those dolts,
those chumps, those harebrains and babbling fragments.
How terrible it must be, condemned to
childhood without knowing it, without fear.
They circled our games shyly, hung apelike
from the monkey bars, laughing at the dirt.
A blow on the head could do it, I knew,
a car crash, football game, angry brother—
I could be sentenced to endless field trips,
to handicrafts and conveyor belt jobs.
I could be happy with TV forever.

I did not pray then and am not praying now,
but let me be lumpish and rude, let me
drift like sawdust out of my ugly clothes,
let my tongue falter and my eyes give way—
anything to avoid that laughter
with screeches of comprehension, that youth
in the dusty light without holiday.
I may be foolish but I'm not fooling—
at cocktail parties, committee meetings,
speaking or taking notes, I see myself
in every lamebrain who chokes down a laugh.

Breaking and Entering

I liked the smell of insecticide,
how it leaked from sloppy tank trucks
rumbling into our neighborhood
on obscure charters. They left blue tire treads
across intersections, blue smudges on grass,
and a sweet blue smog in the air.
One by one the grandfather elms were sprayed.

I liked those tree men, brusque or sheepish,
when they came door to door
in poison overalls, warning mothers
to hide their children inside, for it was dangerous
as fallout. Did anyone believe?
How could they, watching those workmen
covered head to boot with blue smut?

I liked all sorts of storied danger,
from the hail that dented an uncle's golfcart
and left him hoarse with God's praise,
to the lightning that flattened my mother,
skinnydipping in her own childhood.
I liked my brother sneaking home late,
the drunken clank of car keys on his dresser.

I liked those TV families slamming their doors,
how half an hour solved everything.
When their phones rang I always would answer.
In our house there was no rashness, no resolution.
A skulker in those nights, I liked to pry open windows
locked shut—abandoned shacks, garages,
toolsheds stocked with musty canvas lawnchairs.

But once in, I only wanted out.
My courage reduced to jimmied locks, nails eased back
into their holes. I must have been searching
some better privacy. And one day
I stood in a vacationing neighbor's living room,
mad for secrets. I turned every cushion,
pulled every drawer, found nothing worth looking for.

Companion of Dusk

Uncle Gray stood in the door, letting in flies,
his crookback body a gargoyle of pain:
"What, am I Christ? I should suffer gladly
like some lost idiot in a movie?"

I was a kid, but that doesn't help much,
watching someone else come to die, pill bottle
in a spasming hand, man I barely knew
arguing with my mother over pain

and what it allows. I invent this tale
out of a bent need to say love, to star
in my own life by making another's,
rising from each as from basement gunfights

with my brother. Once, stunt-rolling downstairs,
I whacked my head on the floor and *saw stars,*
I rose sparkling and aflame like crossed wires
and wouldn't play dead for a good weekend.

I hated you, Uncle Gray, for your pain.
I hated your going crazy knowing
what everyone knows, that we die, that it hurts,
when it hurts, alone. You were no movie.

My tied tongue loosened, your crumpled dollar
pressed into my hand, our memory sweet
as spirits on ice: no salve for these wounds.
When the body shudders and fails, the mind

often follows, for though the mind's better
it is not different from. Would I taste hope
like a story on my tongue? You didn't.
You set your last mark like a cigarette

on the air, orange nothing, companion
of dusk, a star flaring into its own end.
In your guest room you took it easy—
who now must rest without peace, my guest star.

Boys and Fireworks

All night they've praised night
with explosions below my window
followed by giddy laughter.
Happiness is wrong, I want to say,
with my headache, with my insomnia,
but these boys are without form
and won't hear above the splintering hiss
and crack echoing down our hill
and up Paris Mountain. Besides,
happiness is not wrong, just annoying,
like a secret date or a change
in the menu. Catcalls and horselaughs—
the boom of my own building
withstanding all. A light, cool rain
settles like breathing dust,
and I wander the white noise of sleep
for whole minutes until, with snorts
of warning, another volley sparkles
over the hayfield. Tonight
I'd almost welcome the mockingbird's
bad jokes, anything but this
separate piece of the world
flaring like mad fireflies. I know these kids,
their nicknames and bravado,
one eye out for the searchlight
of the cops. As a kid I too
wanted to ignite the brick-by-brick
hush of a sleeping world,
wanted all the more because
nothing came of it but movies
I played against the dim treeline
of my truant dreams. And all I did
was dress up dogs, burn anthills,
camp out in my own backyard
where I watched the TV glimmer
of my parents' bedroom until

it expired. Tonight, standing in my
underwear on the balcony, I squint
upon the dark, seeing nothing
but the manic slice of a bat's wing
across my light. I'm sad now
those kids have been spooked quiet
by someone, not me. I won't say
I miss their idiot joy. Sadness
is not wrong, just regret.

Grimmer than the front page,
knotted spidery in some corner—
there must be reason for these thoughts,
some way out of memory
that's not up through vapid windows
or down yesterday's ruined steps.

Rick Zavada sang for years
in St. John's choir, sang over
the minister, sang right.
One Saturday night he chased
his frail, churchless father
down Main Street with a snow shovel,
battering three pool hall loafers
as they disarmed him. Everyone
nodded, had seen this coming
or something worse—knew it
by Rick's translucent skin,
his funeral-parlor mincing
at coffee hour, white shirt and bow tie
he wore by choice to school.

Then, rumors of a hospital
where Rick was tamed, and good
again. Three more months
he sang among us, eyes uplifted
and glazed with such joy
few could bear his unblinking.
But this time it was a jack handle
and his father would not run again.
Rick rode that patrol car into our minds
and wouldn't leave, even when we prayed
him away, even when we tried
singing in his crazy tenor.

I remember one Sunday
the church basement flooded—
Rick went down barefoot
with rolled pants into the stale gloom

as if on his last mile to Lourdes.
He brought us all our vestments.

No one's descended those stairs
in years without seeing Rick,
his moonface reflected
in murky waters. Stained glass martyrs
still muse on the creaky choir,
lacking its one clear voice—and who
could say he's not glad it's gone?

There must be reason—dead fathers
still sprint down Main Street nightmares.
There must be some generous spleen
to preach Rick's bad news well.
Here comes that boy, we say,
we knew it a long while ago.
Yes, we saw him coming, but not
when or how—the robes he wore
we put on and removed in silence.
He was the still water we knew
ran in our own veins, so cool
it feels hot, so quiet it reads
the least ripple of life as death.

Which Rick was most himself?
Was he driven on by our blameless tongues?
I think, gone haywire, he was immune
to us, not us to him—this boy pitiful
and still dangerous, whose father
will neither die nor stop dying.
Like rain on the roof, we say,
Rick Zavada is monotonous grief.
Like April snow in the gutter
he's grown different from himself.

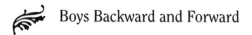

"You take the language, I'll keep the fur"
—from a dream

Let's roll this whole movie backwards
and see swimmers sucked along feet first
by their thrashing wakes, silly grins vanishing
under inverted splashes, then feet and legs
arcing up softly to the quivering board
where they'll bounce a bit, then retreat, retreat.

Where do they go, those glistening selves
tanned and dripping with their yawning summers?
Why are they climbing into cutoffs and T-shirts
with such eager faces? Why would they scatter
backwards down the driveway on wobbly bikes?

Already the June leafage is draining away
into paler shades of May and April.
The last freak snowfall mushrooms over brown grass
before fluttering upward. Soon we will reappear
clumsy-legged among snowbanks, catching snowballs
and disassembling them carefully back to our feet.
We'll be just faces now, peering out
from the hoods of our fur-lined parkas,
and everyone will be busy swallowing
cloud after cloud of indigestible words.

The Attic Which Is Not Desire

This storehouse of fractured whims,
best room in the house, grand view,
past or present, whose skimpy windows
shepherd light around webbed corners
without crimp, without cozening—

Someone peering from the lacy avenue
would glimpse at most a pale face,
half-lit moon wheeling across
dimming pane, no sooner seen
than gone—one name flashing
in a thumbed book, one spear of sun
from some distant turning car.

From the attic, December light slants
across the hemmed yards like a leg
over a double bed. Forsythia blooms
in unseasonal heat, beautifully doomed
and fit to be described. The neighborhood
recedes into the future, new pop tunes
peeling out in gravel driveways,
children of friends sprouting beards and breasts
to the hard look in my canny eye.

The high bedroom of the house opposite,
yellow with sour hope, dusk everlasting,
was once the flick and glimmer
from my fingertips' pale candles.
Now desire's planted and strewn with dust
here amid fusty deer heads, rifle parts,
dresses stiff with long-changed minds.

Nostalgia's reek is not sad, just mild,
faithful, nosy—and no room for it anymore.
Among this trussed estate, given second wind
like the winter fly battering this chill swath
of light across the sill, won't I want out
without knowing what that means? I will and do.

1.
Whose boat capsized in bait-strewn waters?
Who felt the rasping curiosity of

a shark? Who became bait amid bait?
Two hunters scrabbled into emptied beer coolers

(imagine the fumbling, teetering haste of it)
—rode them all day like coffins afloat.

Was it a passing trawler saw them waving?
All the time, they said, sharks nosed

and swirled, scratching the fiberglass
with their cinderblock hides. Did they sing,

and if so, was it hymn or alma mater?
Or did they swear the cursed poverty

of words? The bait was soon gone,
blood dissolved in kelp, in the wrack

from their upturned hull. Were waves high?
They saw them so. All they'd learned

returned: do not thrash the water,
and when nudged by that idiot snout,

kick squarely and hard, which sometimes works.
Once begun, a harsh line of thought

will not easily disperse in fertile waters.
Imagine then telling tales to swallow fear,

to say what happened. Living to tell,
I swear, the cursed poverty of words.

2.
Memory is the telling, not the tale.
From a rising plane green-black water vanishes,

showing only sand, comfortable brown
when light is right. The water I feared

all children love in dread, to go in it, go down
or be pulled there by the snapper

alive in family legend, that rose
to a cousin's taunting, greenbacked

rock, and clipped a toe away,
trickling blood soon lost in the waves.

Or: to ride the glass-bottomed boat
shoulder to shoulder with friends

seeing the underworld as a garden
with purple sea fans waving in our wake,

staghorns, knots of deadman's fingers,
blue crabs and orange stars—and suddenly

a shark dull as sand, that without
trying or knowing turns all boats

henceforth glassy and thin keeled.
A boy riding his father's back

snorkeling along the coral reef
feels the bottom's lure, its shape-shifting

power—even before his joking father
dives for the bottom as if stung by air.

3.
Learning to swim: first you conquer
natural panic, dunk your face, blow bubbles,

finally open eyes. That strangeness you forget
is real, the water never more alien

than when you learn to trust it. Still,
you dream of death by common water,

swimming pool, storm drain, lilypad pond—
the bottom a magnet, a mouth

delivering you down. A hum
in your ears they swear is only blood.

4.
At sunset the family lake's a bowl of deceptions:
plonk of a jumping fish, paired swallows merging,

voices lazy and blurred drifting from a canoe
too far to see in the silvery glare

that reddens, heaving mountains higher,
cooling the sand to the color of bats.

This is the ocean that tugs my lungs
in the night, on whose speckled shore-stones

the belly-up perch still rests, drawing dogs,
lake where a waterlogged tree has lain

for twenty summers in the oakey muck, one stub
of a limb long enough to just brush

the legs of a swimmer. Once a neighbor planted
a six-foot stuffed swordfish on that beach

to puzzle the retrievers. The stiff bristle
of a few reeds in the shallows gave the lie

in the joke photo we took—though on whitecap days,
from low enough, this lake becomes the sea.

5.
A boy and his brother, old enough
to run an outboard but too small to go far,

invent a game called "pearls before swine,"
after their mother's favorite expression.

The pearls are gobs of lake mud,
rank and black hitting the air—and they

must dredge up two handfuls apiece to stay in.
Anchoring the skiff in ten-foot water, they begin.

Then when both have smeared the hull's
dented aluminum with black palm prints,

they anchor deeper and deeper. Like all
worthy games, this has real penalties:

lung-crushing weight of deep water,
ears aching in the surprising cold,

but most of all the fear that kicks in
like an outboard just when they dig bottom

in that blind murk, and up to see
the wavering silhouette of their hull

smaller than it should be. Though swimming up
is easier than down, it's also harder.

Part II

Self-Portrait with Stage Fright

This isn't my real personality
standing up half casually
to talk about myself. Usually
I'm sparrow-skittery,
shy as water through
my own fingers—
just ask my mother,
if you can find her; that's her
hunched in the back row
or two steps from the door.

Usually dew glazes my lip
when everyone's looking,
sleet thrums my stomach,
a regular hailstorm
in my knees.

What can I give you
but dark inklings
you already know
or a twinge or two
out of history? What is
my stammering hello
but code for farewell?

Wouldn't you rather watch
buzzards circle their roosting tree?
Without past, without regard
they swirl as black snowflakes
in one of those bubble villages
that live on coffee tables.

Shake them and they perform.
Shake me and I'm gone.

Self-Portrait with Australia

I'm tired of Australia, always so far,
always long sandy roads to nowhere ranches,
great barrier reef swallowing prime ministers,
always its thick lager, its parallel cowboys.
Who's not tired of that rusty accent and bloody
    vocabulary?

A rock star might fancy Australia
for its stony shell and emptiness within,
its wrong constellations, its largeness, its smallness,
even its backward drains. Not me.
I spit upon the marriage of the seas.
I forget Cockatoo Island, Wollongong, and Lake
    Disappointment.
The *National Geographic* can have its hypocrite bikinis
in Melbourne, in Perth, its heaped fruitbaskets
and plucky minor airlines going down.

If in Australia the sun goes cockeyed,
if the vistas and sinks enchant tourists,
I'll give up my marsupials, my rabbits,
for sheep-haunted stretches of stretched mind.
From dingo to wombat, I'm unimpressed
with that convict sprawl—for all I care
Captain Bligh may live there forever, fending off
    mutinies.

In my father's study I first greased my fingertips
on the beachball globe that wobbled spinning
on its invisible pivot. Postage stamps, topographies,
revolutions without boundary: after arctic denial,
after martyrdom in the red countries,
no plumbing or medicine in the green ones,
Australia's aboriginal vacancy was room for any boy.
It was Texas without Alamo, where the words came easy.

But goodbye boomerang wisdom, hello goldfinch and garbage
    truck.
Give me the underland of my own distress.

The Day I Cannot Stop Crying

Speck dazzling one eye, lens glint of sun,
maybe fumes from underground engines
that power our day—whatever it is,
my nerves know this blur will last daylong,
fogging half my hours, a grief without source.

Let the turning maple swim, red and rust,
in my right eye—my left has no time
for this driveling riddle, this *Weltschmerz.*
I read the news with proper irony,
tidal waves against the crisp columns
of disaster, treaty, and no comment.
I'm half inclined to resurrect my soul
from its lifelong torpor, to float my sins
and almost hurl myself down that dark well.

Clogged tear duct? Partial allergy? Remnant
of sorrow, lodged at last where I cannot
think it away? This welling semi-world
would seem too deep for tears were it not
lovingly abrim, and I feel Yes and No
at war within, like a father seeing
his truant son take a deserved beating.

Do I sadden because I am crying
or vice versa? Do I worry the rage
of every smudged headline? Someone does or
does not slice an onion in my bad kitchen,
and I know the beam in my eye is a mote
in the camera lens of history.
But I won't cry for that. I cry despite
myself, and not because rain is the sweat
of the damned, not because good citizens
must climb their roof crests to ride out the flood
of this last hurricane's one-eyed blinking.

To the north the thunderheads thicken—
bikinis and tennis weather to the south.

Why, when the metal of responsible life
lies sweet in its sheath, must I know this split
that is itself half pain, half theatric?

I cry with half a heart that one whole eye
takes in the world's wind, refusing to blink.

Unguided Tour of Floyd, Virginia

Any man, anywhere could be a Floyd—
not a Grundy, Fancy Gap, Pulaski,
and not Galax, Bland, or Independence.
In Floyd even the dogs would be friendly,
curled on stoops, too lazy to wag their tails,
but wrinkling their eyebrows in welcome.
There'd be no cash registers in this town—
the waitress at the Hello There Cafe
reaches into her well-traveled pockets
to bring, without counting, my exact change.
The Chevrolet dealer gives me a car
to test drive, refusing to inspect
my license or note my name—and hands me
a twenty to get it filled at the self-serve.
In this loose country I find a firm home.
Cows perch like stones on the rocky hillsides
and rain drifts along, one face to the next.
Hard to tell much about rain, hard to care
if the Open sign on that store is a lie.
Any man, anywhere could be David
welcoming this overburdened clothesline
for its brilliance. I'd hang out my own wash
if I had any. I know I am wrong
to linger here, even in admiration.
Aren't all towns the same, from trashy front yards
to whitewashed stones and tires lining driveways?
One town cannot see or hear the next
in these well-folded hills, though people thrive.
They change businesses without changing signs—
the old Gulf station is now a print shop,
despite faded "Feed & Seed" lettering.
The man in charge smiles at my confusion,
saying, "Things change fast in Floyd." I want to
believe him (it would be a friendly thing),
but I cannot help noticing the broom
fallen in a corner, wrapped in cobwebs.

Maybe I used to live here. Maybe Floyd's my home town,
just wrinkled a bit with my bad memory,
a wallet snapshot carried too long.
But I have no business to give or take.
Behind Floyd's picture windows I won't look,
except to spot myself flashing along,
fumbling for an instant as I change gears.

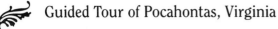 Guided Tour of Pocahontas, Virginia

—for Frank Soos

What can be learned on a one-day visit?
Chances are I'd look all day at rubbish,
thinking it profound, unless some native
guided me into the stories of this town,
a soggy, moss-grown hollow tucked among
hills once rich with coal, now crossed with networks

of shafts and tunnels where dripping water
loosens what remains. I-beams, wooden posts
shore up rock more surely than the markets,
body shops, and houses of beauty
can resurrect days of full employment.
Was it three mines working then, and coal trains

stacked here to Pittsburgh? Was the company
a store too full for a boy to explore?
Now boys toss footballs up and down the streets
as if to show that Thanksgiving supper
was no less, no more than they expected.
And twenty-five years of various schemes

toward prosperity have reduced themselves
to historic markers on the highway.
Was a fortune made here selling coffins?
The price was high. I know an outdoor fire
would sizzle in this gray-black rain—coal dust
everywhere, the creek slowly recovering

with bad times permanent. What can be known
without living here, eating cabbage rolls
in church basements, honing gossip like knives?

What can't memory say? The old train bed,
thick with briars, bottles, and rusted parts
of forgotten machines, sprawls across town

like a paralyzed arm. At the graveyard
on the hill, a splendid view of local
stubbornness—six churches, two black, four white,
all identical to these outside eyes,
all ready to speak in tongues of great loss,
even the Hungarian Catholics

perched on the rock of their protested faith.
The neighborhoods gather around each church
with their identical, company homes
that have outlived the company. Smoke rises
here and there, easily misunderstood
as rage. For there's no money anymore

to keep up the cemetery, which rots,
overgrown with honeysuckle, stones chipped
and toppled, beer cans gathered in circles
around piles of cigarette butts. One crypt,
famous for its faulty top, in good light
gives a view of unambiguous bones

among the blown leaves and trashed dropped in.
In a junkyard a green bus labelled "Christ"
rusts beneath its crumpled roof. The spirit
lives in every cinderblock coal shed, car
overflowing a garage, and Beware
Of Dog sign before a yard without dogs.

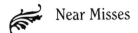 Near Misses

How despite odds, premonitions that flare
and vanish like those sparkling voices
loving us just as we nuzzle to sleep,

we never know when the careening car
of a volunteer fireman, red flasher
off-center on its roof, will almost plane

into us at a stop sign, or a truck
with its cargo of black rain-coated men
may drive us ditchward minutes later . . . .

So we drove, joking wouldn't it be strange,
as now we turned left down the right road
to see tail lights halted where

suddenly we knew they had to be.
Silhouettes in red swirling exhaust
across the open-windowed house: but all

safe, tucked in their coats on the lawn:
family, circle of stunned friends
grown festive, all with wrapped bottles of wine

as if in tribute to this lord of chance.
The chimney spouted flame, cinders spewing
from the dark stalk like ideas from a war.

But fire must finally kill itself.
On the roof spark-defined men gossiped,
aimed flashlights better to see it die.

Soon enough inside, we blew our hands alive,
opening bottles in the pleasant chill
of what didn't happen, its smoky calm

entering all, hair, breath, mind, coats
we piled on their once immaculate bed.
All night stories circulated, but not

the one running behind everyone's eyes
like home movies, fragmented countdown
to flapping white that signals the end:

how sooner or later the night siren,
door knock, telephone call must be
that one we can't imagine or stop

imagining, whose many inklings pass
around a festive table, all vying
to fashion the best anecdote as if

without plan, as if luck were meat and drink,
not smoldering timbers of any home.
So not just wine edged our voices louder,

higher: how last night someone saw
on the same road the sheet-covered figure
of a dead pedestrian, knocked shoeless

by an unlucky car, or yesterday's news
of a man who jumped or was pushed in flames
from a local bridge, glimpsed in midair

by motorists, a meteor to slice
across their hearts before homing
to some original dark and manic

plenitude. Then soon enough, one story
not just leading to another, like roads
from life to life, but *being* each other,

as some age-dazzled couples
grow into static, bickering children
with identical fears. And further back

we talked, the past all twinkling sky
of hit and near miss, the same stars
wheeling, giving shapelessness its shape.

 The Mind's Eye

"We call the moon the moon"
—Donne

We call this night the night,
for sleep is always itself, and dream,
and by the light of habit
our habits are illuminated.

Like light thrown back on itself
until it grows single-minded,
the mind cuts glass, etches steel,
and burns with pure attention.

We call a solo diner a party
of one. The mind's party
is always on, especially when it's late,
it's lonely, and it's crowded with dark.

For fields are different every hour:
light changes more than rain, snow,
the withering harvest. We walk them
expecting to be changed, as we are.

Work, we call whatever it is
we do often or well. We talk,
give thanks, think of reasons
for postponement. We work like hell.

We call despair despair, and a shiver
nothing but. The moon is cold,
we say, frigid ourselves, and searching
a cold beauty. We call the end

the beginning. It is the end.

Loons

1.
I can't remember which loon I chased most—
one in the lily-thick waters of Long Pond,
my father and I backpaddling hard,
wrong again, those chuckles rising at our back

—or the loon I got from Thoreau,
that "stately bird" eluding his boat
for one whole afternoon and three pages,
not resisting "demoniac laughter"
at his methodical pursuer, in fact
giving away his position laughing
the instant he surfaced. "He was indeed
a silly loon," wrote Thoreau, who shared
my father's mordant turn of the bow.

We were deeper in the woods than Thoreau
at Walden, with his lunchbasket hauled
from town. But we had come in a turquoise
motor home with my mother, brother,
and two spaniels more spooked by the woods than we.
All night they cringed beneath the chassis
and wouldn't budge as the ratchety laugh
and coyote howl of a pair of loons
washed over our little patch of shoreline.

2.
We chase but cannot fathom. It was years
before I knew that manic laughter
as not mirth but alarm—nest in danger,
hunters on the shore, some fool and his Dad
canoeing close to the chicks. Years
till I learned what a marvellous
patch-and-paste job was *Walden,* boiled down

from the Journals like gallons of maple sap
to a cupful of perfect syrup.
Years before I learned to welcome
the five or six anecdotes my father
let surface from his past—into the wind,
into rain-stippled waters where we all swam.

Loons can dive with a yelp and splash
but sometimes just sink without ripple
to swim whatever way you're not looking.
Long Pond's waters are shallow and black,
strewn with lily pads from the shoreline in,
halting only at a patch of clear water
at the center, where loons will stay as long
as need be. My father mapped the water for me.

3.
It's never easy to gauge depth, or time,
its nocturnal wailing, its daylight
splashing brilliance that blinds. I'm trying
to chase down the loons we paddled over
and ones I had to search on my own,
bolstered by books and this skittish love of fact.

For water takes color wherever it can—
starched green of early fall hardwoods,
sprinklings of red, bark and bud, yellow
of early turnings, and over it all
the varied froth of sky, milky to ice-green.

And bottom silt, so many browns it grows
murky as good tweed, laced with twigs, turbid
trashy nests. With all this definition
you'd think water could be photographed
but no—just then clouds would part, broken

upon a spear of sun, and water would shiver
as if with a waft of striders,
wind wrinkling the flat skim
until what we behold is not water
but our own eyes darting, glimmer and glint,
so bright it is all sky and sky beyond sky.

Water gets these stones by heart, drops branches
across its own broad back, yet says nothing,
not even a warning not to construe.
A loon says more, though we interpret wrongly
each wail, tremolo, or yodel upon
time-stunned waters. How I heard my first one
that humid August night—coyote howl
tapering to some madman chuckling—
eased from doglike cringing by my father's talk.

4.
Still I return wordless but rich with names
to the scurrying, endless reunion
of water, my homing instinct for this pond
I've seen just twice in twenty years since.
Still the blank slate of its sunblind water,
and the same or a new pair of loons bristling
in the waves a hundred yards out. Wind
at our backs, we can't hear a thing yet
but our own voices dispersing like clouds.
We paddle out in a new canoe, not
to chase but to savor—(to a loon it looks
the same). What we write upon the water
with our paddles, the wind still erases.
What we write again, after dark at the fire
of stories told and retold, remains.

 Wedding Gift

Why can't I remember my long walking?
Maybe pebbles went rolling underfoot,
maybe I startled to a dog's lunging,
maybe one day the rain drove slantwise
like these thoughts I shake off, and stand dripping.

It may have been hard going, I don't know.
This weariness feels like some sad pleasure,
as if I had proved something. But what?
To tramp all this way without an address?
To stumble over a bare threshold grinning?

It is the house of my oldest friend—
now marrying a woman I don't know.
The orchids in her hair give no odor
that I can tell. Her smile that's not for me
plays upon his dream-lit face like a flame

unburning. Yet haven't I brought blessings
for them both? Isn't the smudged mug of pink tea
in my hand a gift? When he looks my way
at last, I say, "It's cold, and I drank half
myself." Neither of us can stop laughing.

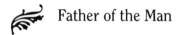

Your daughter, fifteen, has drunk a half bottle
of gin, passing out in the bushes.
Her boyfriend's car costs twice what your first house did.
Blood of your blood, heart root blossoming,
still she does not figure in this story.

For a more bitter car now squeals away.
The hair you've lost is not entirely gone:
see, it returns on your son's clenched jaw
as he plays air guitar in his bedroom,
his walls all Nazi regalia, his dreams
all wind-stunned and far from this sick village.
Yes, here is the hard seed you recognize.

No, he won't go to the ballpark with you.
He's tired of your beery friends, your tapedeck
spewing sixties junk, throbbing blue vein
rising on your temple. And old? He's never
seen such a decrepit father, when you've
tipped a few and begun leering at
the available wives, sometimes even
stripping your shirt off for volleyball. . . .

And you know that *grump grump* bass that rises
all evening from his basement hideout?
It's nothing but your sullen, well mapped fate.
It's all those wind-in-the-blood whiskey nights
you vowed never to forget or regret.
It's dust spraying as you popped your wheelies
through the vacant lot that's now a realtor's.

It's the open legs of your dream at last
beckoning—no, you can't leave her out now—
her prom-night giggle and hushed, skinnydipping
waters you still feel throb in your belly.
Bass and drum, the synthesized wail rising
to the night trees—father, it's all you ever
hoped or could be, this welcome capsizing
and perfect acquittal. This shutout game
you'd never have trusted when you were your age.

The Valley Where We Live

A doe stands in the garden, nibbling lettuce
we don't care to pick. OK, we say to the sun.
Between the deer's legs rabbits walk their awkward way.
The valley where we live is steep but not cloistered.
Anything mild may enter: rain showers,
balloons, snails, dictionaries, timothy, milk.
Any born violence soon rises of its own energy
and spins off the rim of our horizon.
We make up gentle nicknames to their memory:
dust devil, hooligan, zigzag, roughhouse.
Potatoes turn earth itself sweet, we say,
burying our mild dead where we must.
We like poplar trees, how they take the quaking wind
and calm it with slender semaphore.
Sometimes, though, wandering the upper paths,
we hear from beyond our valley muffled shouts,
insistent chant of engines run uphill.
Then the poplars shudder without wind.
Then we pace our sheep-cropped lawns meaning to do
whatever we have forgotten. Like children
standing the first time at a cliff's windy edge
we wonder what it is keeps us from leaping.

Why I Love Halloween

I live in Eden, a small town
south of Buffalo, New York,
whose major talent is departure.
Fogged windows reveal messages
from last season's travelers,
such as *badly needed rest*
and *forgive only the cold.*
Waiting for the tournament bus
a basketball team stands
under a streetlight, among puffs
of breath, seeing everything
as performance. Half our streets
are split for an overdue sewer.

Oh, a small town wind
can turn black and bitter,
can polish even stop signs blank.
How small a town should get
is a question for the second page
of the agenda, following
our honored guest, Coach Something,
who will offer toasts
to his boys young and old,
who will show a movie
and then study his lap
as the Lutheran pastor rises
to bless all with watery eyes.

Even so, today my bank teller
gives me candy corn and speaks
encouragement into the microphone
as she pushes money in a tube.
With green face, blue lips,
bedraggled antennae, she reminds me
of my favorite adjective: *lurid.*
Best of all, her boss, ridiculous

in cowboy hat and timid moustache,
looking determined to be a sport.
And everywhere, people nodding
and smiling, all out of hope
and decent proportion.

Self-Portrait as Author and Citizen

Any phone book or card catalog
shows me my half dozen or more other selves:
some disguised by different middle names,
some taking refuge entirely in initials,
but all betraying the reek of selfhood
that cannot deny its own. I have written a book
on reincarnation, another on the religious lives
of country music stars, and several
on the enigmas of cellular development.
I can even call myself and ask
when I'll be getting home, and the woman who answers
is my wife without knowing it, a fact more comforting
than it ought to be. Sometimes I'll chat
with my child or roommate, but it's a thin charade:
I know all my social security numbers when added
would total some prime number, *one* to its best power,
as I have noted in my treatise on algebraic philosophy.

Whenever I vote I stand in the world's shortest line
in a waiting room just off the municipal courtroom,
where a gray-haired woman I've seen somewhere before
asks my name and repeats it to another woman
in a voice loud enough to ruffle the curtains
of the voting booths. Then she places
a fat black pencil line through each responsible letter
of the name and address I claim.

Part III

Letter from London

Traffic rivers nowhere to nowhere,
never the same twice, preserved
like a face caught once in a crowd

and ever returning, those liquid eyes
curious a moment, fleet smile,
then the slow-congealing look

of *being seen.* I wander through
these chartered streets marking fair skin
and crooked vowels of my forebears,

the scuffed-suitcase taxicabs
skittering down mazes each driver
must keep in his head. Everything seen

or heard comes with its own label:
remember this. What to preserve?
Trafalgar Square, with its stumblebum

searching the cracks on all fours?
St. Paul's? It's impossible
to fix a monument—though ravens

at the Tower, symbols of permanence,
sport clipped wings. Guy wires on the bridge
are tuned by wind to a note

I feel yet don't hear, like the cool air
that precedes a train down the underground.
Later, a scrawl of accents on the sidewalk,

workmen on a scaffold singing—
clipped, welcome surge of the mother tongue,
as behind floor-to-ceiling curtains

at the hotel I murmur even older words
into my muffling pillow. Silly enough:
to savor the tune of *pub, lorry,*

petrol, the way a girl on the bus
leans into my question and says "sorry?"
To love even that difference familiar

from books, films, and television,
as a husband will relish the pale surety
of his wife's body. To love most

the word I can't fathom or pronounce—
how it flashes down a lane, just missed,
or floats an instant on public airwaves,

heard by the nodding watchman
if caught at all. Not a delicious word
superior to all, but simply the one

I am listening for. A one-man band
echoes off dingy tile near tube escalator.
Hat at his feet, he wails American blues,

nodding as I toss in my dollar
among the alien coin. His buried voice
rings with cocky despair: "Nobody knows

the trouble I seen. There's people
in the poorhouse doing better than me."
O Leadbelly, Mississippi John,

Big Joe Turner—I know this ain't
nobody's business but my own,
how I search the air for your next chord,

how I taste each word like a schoolboy
love his pie, how in my rented room
I will play and replay your dateless news.

Kinds of Jazz

One song says it right: a whole lotta shakin's
going on: upheavals in other lives
I read about with bagel and coffee
before I pack my briefcase and forget
my way to work. When I ask my students
who Joseph Stalin was, or when World War I
ended, I get row upon row of blanks.
And these are people, I complain to friends
in barrooms, who know every World Series
like a catechism, who know to the cent
how much an engineer or lawyer makes.
Am I much different? I know each song
the Beatles recorded, but could not give
any clear apology for my life.
History comes with its own radio:
haunted tunes I recall as year of war,
year of riots, year of school or marriage.

I listen for history's jazz, but the music
of what happens is a poor thing compared
to the great as if, which is music jazzed
beyond reproduction. One night I heard
a blues guitar so fine it was like
a dentist's drill full of love, a conversation
between one scripture and the next.
That man onstage in his blue suit,
that corny, fat father of the beer
commercials, played his jive so hard it came
true, right there in the smoky spotlight where
I'll never be. I loved even his jazz
between numbers, jokes old enough to shine.
I take that night's improvisation as fact:
scat sung well replenishes thin voices.
I loved how a phrase, left hanging by
the trumpet, would be gathered in his hands
and strung like a spiderweb in the light.

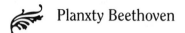 Planxty Beethoven

Where better to worship music than church—
sanctuary amid sanctuary?
Above us, some incense of desire swirls
mindful and apart. Call it a lost bat,
circling this quartet as counterpoint,
as jazz dissolving their surging measure.
At first no one sees the looping presence
in the dusky rafters where, other nights,
all eyes might focus, driven upward
by words—but soon enough we feel quickened
and succumb to names: bat trapped in the slow
movement rising tidelike toward its own shore.
It clings to the altar a while, then bursts
into a tonic chord in the scherzo
and now dodges whatever's above us
we can't see. Some watch his light notes
written on air, some close eyes or concentrate
on their feet, but these four players merely
grin drawing Beethoven out of the same
flickering air. In the intermission
the cellist says he'd like to hear music
with bat ears: useless, maddening desire.
Violinist says nothing useless is desired.

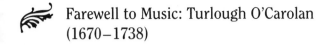 Farewell to Music: Turlough O'Carolan
(1670–1738)

Stone blind, drunk, blind as Homer,
blind as musical gab must be,
O'Carolan harped his way across
the land Cromwell had reconciled.
Not lordly as the ancient dead,
this smallpox-scarred composer:
he remains a drifting voice
over bogland and hummocked pasture
where he never strolled, humming airs.

   Where are the Irish women
   who kissed and romped before?
   Gone, lost with their lovenames,
   their very bones dissolved.
   But one beauty smiles across their sky,
   across many a quill-scratched page.

He did his keening in the great houses,
pouring flattery's whiskey
recklessly upon fire-warmed stone.
No servant didn't know his kindness
or fear his scalding tongue.
Drunk on his deathbed, he rolled
to the floor, singing to all—
"It takes a great man to fall lying down."

But rooks cry, circling sea cliffs,
some car squeezes down a lane to the pub,
and no royalty pays anyone for song.
We pay ourselves instead, over and over—
I think of the country jukebox I saw,
where you could purchase silence itself
at twenty-five cents a minute.

Blind earth, blind sky, blind tune
one part surf spray, one part seaweed
flung upon uncomprehending rock.

Yes, she twirls in baroque petticoats
and high-stacked wig, yes, we nod yes
long after she has skipped away.

For we know her hand—would know it
a lifelong dream away. Saddle the horse,
tune the balky harp—it takes
a great man to orchestrate his dying.

Planxty Beatles

"Beneath the blue suburban skies"

My radio goes wrong: an old song
cuts loose this night, arriving
like wind that shakes the cornstalks
as I drive from one darkened town
to another, from house of birth
to house of marriage. I grope for the dial
to clarify. Then comes a tide
of ten-year-old patter, ads
for dead companies, movies
whose titles echo vanished slang.

Yet it is song, song fading
and swelling with these back roads,
that keeps me awake tonight,
that sweeps like my headlights
over the trembling clotheslines
and moonstruck farm ponds,
wedging a delicate arc into the past.

Nothing to do but drive on
though the songs grow younger still,
though they drift and bleed together
and slip into other tongues.
At the fringes of a town
I know by heart, a few house lights awaken,
bedroom to bathroom to yellow kitchen.
A mailbox dented by some winter's plow
floats into sight to the manic, brassy tune
of "Penny Lane," though for a moment
it looks more like my startled face.

 Planxty Charles Ives

How many buttons on your coat, Grandpa,
and are they brighter than mine?
Do they gleam like stars in the flag?
Go out at sunset to reel down the colors
that night would only bleach and burn.
No ice cream social now, no tea time,
no doilies riding the arms of our chairs.
This is the future, friends, not the past.
For a man plans, he has insurance,
even if starlings come roost in his brain,
scattering at the gunshot of dawn.
It's not pretty, a man's dream—just how it is,
stiff as a moldering photograph
in these days before candids,
when with one hand on a wide lapel
and the other on a horsehead cane
he posed near the opened, unread Bible.
Let us bring in the sheaves, Grandpa,
whistle Dixie to beat the smoothest band,
and listen all the time to the milkwagons
clattering up the green cobblestones of time.

Planxty Lee Morgan

From windy shrieks of subway platforms,
battered basement nightspots and their heat,
from the bedrock stoplight figuration
and the solo dazzle of taxicabs,
from swapping places at the lead mike
until bad is good and midnight is noon,
when eighteen-bar choruses fill
soup-stained airwells, windows always open,
song rising untended as thistle—
from anywhere in this vertical city
the darting bird path of memory,
beat steady as steps on the stairs,
mother's heart deep in her Sunday coat.

Not neon glitter, not headlong odor—
just that crushed metal and dented plans
fall and are lifted up again,
nothing lost, even in the junkyard,
nothing ever wasted at all.

Part IV

Sure

answer to a student

You ask is it boring, sex with the same woman
a decade and more? Could you imagine
a thousand nibbles on the same casserole?
Could you feel wind in your face, a million
rusty afternoons? Maybe it's boring like food
and breeze, and perhaps it's sometimes like tying shoes
or shouldering the front door, especially
when all those heartbreaking others jitterbug
down the street in the filmiest gowns
of will, all those evergreen eyes,
the sun-polished lakewater of their skin.
Surely I've bedded as many of them
as she has conjured ghostly other me's.

Yet poised halfway down the slide to age,
looking each way bewildered, more and more
I stare longingly onward. For the old in love
have something for the young to mock, it frightens
you so, comic to your apple-firm eyes,
your early spring tartness between the legs.
Of course you see mainly disobedient flesh
quivering to rise, the horrid slackness
at elbow and chin, set lines around creased mouths.
I'm not too old to remember that.

And I could say the engorged and laden heart's
invisible to you, with your tidy chemicals,
your small buds, and the night blooming you miss
you miss. I might admit I'm sure, largely drained
of my secrets, the surprise party long past.

But then you'd expect me to turn and praise
waning light on the oak leaves, their heavy
rustling in the late breeze. It would feel right,
watching me step slowly into dusk water.
I won't. Though I'm young enough to want to,
I'm old enough now just to feel evening stir,
every breath now touched with second wind.

 Rough Air

A mile into the sky our plane is
practically nothing. This turbulence
of air—also nothing, like the loose cells
that float within the eye.
Connecticut rolls and pitches below—
Einstein was right, mistrusting his own feet,
and so was Bishop Berkeley, for a plane
glinting unseen among leaden clouds,
droning toward the Atlantic unheard,
is no plane at all, a trick of wind
or blood fevering in the ears.

I'd say to the earth, *look up;* I'd say
to myself, *look down*—but this ride
across nothing rouses the nothingness
in my belly, as the country below
turns to propellor-whipped gray froth.

I'd say we have no fear worth mentioning—
we are a mile above and far below
the parallel lines of time. Instead, I grip
your hand and conjure our bed,
its landscape of tossed sheets, weather
of our mornings there with light diffusing
through venetian blinds—parallel lines that meet.

 Moon Walk

Paper bag? Beer carton? A splash
of liquid rivers from some crumpled heap
down domed asphalt. Country moonlight
cools the dark puddle
that could be blood, and is—
a possum curled as in sleep
above this spreading map of itself.

"Just playing possum," she says
as we stoop to gaze on moon gray fur,
ropy tail, edge of a pink tongue
between set teeth. No fooling,
though, and no mistake—he's dead,
still fresh at it, no sign yet
of the feasting crow, ant, fly.

Does the breeze of our looking
send one last quiver down its leg?

Then our eyes quicken to the pasture
strewn with dry cattle, heads of steer
and yearling turning moonlike
toward us, and away. Beyond,
near a ruined barn, a quiet car
sits in the timothy, faint green
glowing from its radio dial.

"What the whole world says
is Do Not Disturb," she says, turning
away from their unheard lovesong,
the pasture with its breathing outcrops
of dumb life, its invisible chuckholes
and strands of weed-tangled barb wire,
droppings of many seasons,
open slats of night sky lodged
within the creaky barn—

What can we do? What shall we say
as we turn together to the possum,
pretending it has stirred
or will stir when we walk away?

67

Jesus Never Sleeps

Downstairs neighbors quicken
   each morning before we wake—

Jesus-rock litany, gospel aerobics
   rising through our mattress

like heat from winter's
   sullen garden.

Their joyful noise banishes fat.
   I see them toned

and electric as the guitars
   they haul to weekend revival,

trim and unflappable
   as game show hosts.

What blameless sport, to feel
   the beat in your bones

and call it God! Here
   to declare moral joy

in these corruptible bodies,
   these latter days.

Our sleep, though—we cannot
   love another's glee

rousting us from languid
   heartfast dreams,

and blear as we are we curse
   each tribal thump.

Yet who if not some antic god
   unglues our eyes, opens

our mouths to sabbath naming,
   and thrusts these two

nonbelievers into their own
   bodies' good news?

The Fox, a Most Cat-like Dog

Sleek as water and tough as weed
he vanishes from my headlights
like a memory of the woods:
one April day, light burning through
the trees, your hair, the sodden leaves

underfoot, then suddenly
a pool of skunk cabbage below,
huge snow-burning salad of life
that, when bruised, smells all rot
and draws the early flies: you turned away

and I saw the orange of your coat
flicker behind some black willows:
then the city, that wilderness
of fox breath and sly vanishing,
where unleashed dogs prowling a park

slice their pads on smashed bottles, nails,
pop tops: but the fox ascending,
his tail-whisk a puff of exhaust,
tire squealing his full throated cry
that rides dirty air: he doesn't

want out, for he is in and out
and over and above like air,
as even in the all night store
he browses one aisle over,
dog-earing the skin magazines,

knocking to the floor soda cans
no one can find: measly backyards,
then, strongholds of jay and grackle,
where the cat hunting at sunset
catches rusty light in his fur:

he is and is not the same fox
who escaped my dogged headlights,
Love: no terrified, gentle deer
and no brutal, scavenging bear,
this fox I know and cannot say.

Self-Portrait as Lucky Man

Because I pay my bills on time
and often smile when signing checks
my credit limit's been raised again.

I'm looking better and better
these days in the bathroom mirrors
of interstate highway rest stops—

my pallor and road-dazzled eyes
lend me the cool intelligence
of actors in foreign movies

where no one completes a sentence.
And though I cannot find a job
I'm the kind of man you would think

should have no trouble. Yesterday
my car stalled at a traffic light
in time to avoid being hit

by an escaping felon's truck.
Even when I lower my eyes
in pain or shyness I'm sure to glimpse

five-dollar bills in the gutter.
My wife is so kind I do not
deserve her, though she swears I do.

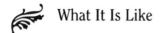 What It Is Like

It is like entering a room to find
Duke Ellington snapping fingers with a grin.
It is like waking up to see an owl
watching you, perched on a bedpost.
No, it is not surprising, though it is
far from dull, like a dog wiggling with joy
to see you after an ordinary day.
It is like sunburn and like the soothing cream.
You hear it just before the first song begins
and in that moment when one cricket
gives up for the night, then another begins,
as though the whole universe were planned
and on schedule . . . .
     Yes, it is like this
and that, but it is not miscellaneous.
Rather, it is like a refrigerator
so full the party could last a week.
You can find it alone, but it is better
with a friend, like watching a TV show
so bad it grows hilarious, and it is good
if you're both playful with it and serious—
like the neighbor you find camped one morning
on your welcome mat, scanning the sports page
of your paper. It is like your welcome mat,
though the letters have worn off with use.
If you are lucky it is like a lightbulb
burning miraculously for at least twelve years.
Even if you are not lucky it makes you feel so.

 Hickory Fall

Gladly far from the targets of childhood,
when squirrels dropped like leaves to my slingshot days—
now nuts fall aimless on roof, lawn, gutter,
while squirrels chitter and cluck from the shagbark.

Does what happened stay, or else radiate
out through spiderweb and dew like first
inclination, like sorrow from its nest
of knowings? Little tree rats, my unfriends,
do I parse you like the wind? Almost
unknowing to my old speck of gloom, I would
locate, I would abide. *Together,* I
wish the wind said. *Gathering. Commonplace.*

Yet wind like a mute sailor rides its own
vanishing trail, like lust, like earth turned
in abeyance, black and stubbled for its
final charmed sleep. Wind hard, wind sharp,
it carries on.

        In prodigal sun
the hickories fall, and tapping all night
on my prodigal dark, they drill to bloom.
And what once was my own light, a flint spark
I crowed over like a tenderfoot
of expertise, my glinting soul, my mind,
now gives off this slow and steady heat
even in rain, windfall and ripening.

 First Snow, Wisconsin

Jacketing oak and hickory limbs
   not as lesson
      but fact

alterable and thus comely,
   this gist, this gospel
      of flux and passage.

Yet let's say the bedded world
   rests, and uncork
      a bottle to sing

as if these were snows
   of yesterday reborn
      today. Two inches, three

by noon, swirling atoms
   of Democritus—they lie down
      as we will, soothed

and wishless, out of shift and swarm
   a single shine. First heart,
      let's say we arrived

in the night, smoothed
   by defining moonlight.
      Let's say we accumulate.

 Second Wind

1. BIRD SKULL: A PAINTING BY LEE SHIPPEY
It lies slantwise on a vivid scarf,
creamy, ashen, fog-colored bone
against sunset purple fabric
with petals and pods of lavender
touched orange.

This eggshell-thin cranium
rendered larger than my own—
any act of attention
turns to love? Who would
embrace doubt alone?

Bird beyond vocabulary
whose thoughtless brain
weighs little, flies nowhere
if not in the second wind
of naming.

2. "BECAUSE SUCH FINGERS NEED TO KNIT / THAT SUBTLE KNOT"
Our love at first was simple
flame, rooted in air,
consuming the night.

Now it feels more
the heat from below, tangled
roots our inspiration:

how we learned thorn and weed,
roadside extravagance
of this walk in time.

River of speech, fire in the clay,
second wind of the flesh
cleaving to its own, its other:

what classic humors
let us breathe what we know,
knitting our knot again.

So if I say I love you
it's not all I intend
but what you understand,

transfigured, ripening,
weed among clustered weeds
as I am you are.

3. MEMENTO VIVARI
Yet if bone on this scarf
is fossil action, halted flight,
it's also the life of seeing

for you, painting it,
and for me, reflecting:
fabric so flat it's not even

background but imperial sky, emblem
and taste of Eve and Adam's
communion—the skull rises

from itself, as if our world
were all foreground, all detail,
and air we feel feathering by

is not first speech anymore
but the shaded, intricate,
second wind enduring.

 Dust Events

1.
Dust unto dust, yes, but when ever
according to plan? I think of

a boy who slipped into earth
as if to see his father follow:

call it a freak accident—
how the manhole cover was loosened

by frost, then a just-right step, and he
swivels instantly down the sewer.

A toddler all at once singing *daddy*
from nowhere, what the ancients called

earth's bowels, now the shunted stink
under each city, where a boy

cries out and knows nothing. Father
knows little more, but enough

to call his wife as he flips the cover
and in turn descends. For the boy,

wading sewage, choked howling,
how that disk of light must have

been itself a fright as it blinked,
then darkened with his father.

By the time his mother appears
the skin of earth seems whole, only

muffled and ghastly voices somewhere,
husband and son the twin diamonds

lodged in her throat. And then,
how to tell their reunion, what

77

we call happy ending, properly
sunlit, though fetid and in time comic—

first son, then father rises into
her arms, smeared with the family waste

turned dark and cold as the past itself,
rank with what lies beyond memory.

2.
Dust unto dust, yes, but slowly,
the mud we are, drying little

by little, skin-cracks with age,
dry mouth and wry wit we call

wisdom. That year I lost thirty pounds,
and why? Did I feel the earth less, tugging

me home? The planet takes nothing
personally, as a bird snagged

in upthrust roots of a beached stump
is no less right than one on the wing.

("The unnatural—that too is natural,"
said Goethe.) Birds, then, are my theme?

From seething life to the slower fires
of earth—a bird's feather soars down.

I think of what they called Poverty
Year across New England, 1816,

twelve months of frost—snow in July,
a gray arctic light over all. Robins

nervous all summer, as when the sun
slides behind the moon at midday.

Tell a bird about volcanos, dust
girdling the earth for years, sunsets

unnaturally fine. No bird alive
to remember the Poverty Year when,

in 1883, it happened again:
Krakatoa sent its acres into air,

rock, seed, flesh and bone turned to powder
and sunset, earth eclipsing itself.

Salt rising from the oceans, farmland
turned over, pollution, volcanos,

the Dust Bowl of the Thirties—science
calls these air-colorings "dust events."

Flame, too, brings darkness and error:
ash from the Great Chicago Fire

so clouded the skies that they turned
beyond red to blue. How rare the day

I seem to understand the way
ash, dust, and rain swirl in world-breath

toward life, rare when my bird-brain stops
preening for death. *Krakatoa:* little chirp,

like a laugh, like my human song surviving—
once in a blue moon lets me thrive.

3.
Atoms are the dust no human
can survive parting. The hugest

dust event hasn't happened yet, but will,
if the wind is any indication,

if the fires of history we tend
so shrewdly tell us anything,

if erosion and decay are the rule
and not coincidence. Fire,

they say, leads to ice as surely
as wind shapes earth. Nuclear winter,

they call it, a dust cloud so vast
it chills and chokes and withers us all.

Probably beautiful, such a ruin
as only neglect can build,

as only the distant eye can see.
I think of the reporter

scribbling metaphors above
Nagasaki: "it was a living

totem pole, carved with many grotesque masks
grimacing at the earth." Yes,

it was a geyser, a mushroom,
a headless beast growing its own

new head. It boiled, it flowered,
it rose like a "giant mountain

of jumbled rainbows . . . much living
substance had gone into those rainbows."

Some dust turned forever to light,
traveling starward at predictable

rate, some dust was so heavy
it fell as black rain, ash from

this human volcano. But the dust
I was born to, eight years later,

was called fallout, and rose so fine
it circles the globe to this day.

4.
So my theme is myself. A boyhood
dream: to see assembled at once

all my leavings, all I had consumed
and cast off, hair and shit and toenails

in one huge pile. What a boy's dream
of power, a primitive wish

to be bigger, and more. Or perhaps
worse: the desire to erase time

and be all my selves at once,
gargantuan folly, as though to meet

myself at forty, at fifty, still aglisten
with the dust-free eyes of birth.

But is it folly, this science of self,
measuring our humors as though

to regain the solemn certainties
of Galen, of Hippocrates?

Renaissance Venice that gave us
Galileo's eye for cosmic dust

gave also his friend Santorio,
whose eye peered earthward, fleshward,

till he became our patron saint
of self-regard, father of

metabolism, first man to measure
the unmeasurable fire burning

our clay. His "static chair" was a scale
to calibrate change. He weighed himself

before and after meals, sex, sleep,
exercise, and probably even

a sneeze. He weighed his own piss, snot,
sweat, and hair cuttings, and discovered

it didn't add up. The difference
was "insensible perspiration."

We call it life, flame in our gut,
lust dancing as the dust motes descend.

5.
So does she love me more when I
grow less? Do health and love diminish me?

Like dust seeding raindrops, perhaps,
my dry, irreducible self

was the necessary pearl she knew
in me, and I found in her. How much

does the soul weigh? Santorio
knew: it weighs more than stout heart,

electric brain, and windy lungs
put together. The difference between

love and lust, I know, is like that
between sweat and insensible perspiration.

Once I saw in a magazine
a woman tan everywhere

but the white upthrust mounds of her ass
presented for all. I thought of

the countless baby photos of just
that pose, tacked to cork boards, taped

to refrigerators, slipped in letters home.
So love is this giddy fire

a parent feels for the pink, half-shaped
thing which came of lust and shall return.

We are not dust but the squirm in mud,
this reckoning wail that lives

on dust and ends there, squalling
from its quick and innocent face.

6.
Even when she's away she lingers
in my air, the sheets, her dust I breathe

and would trust in my sleep, stronger
than the stink of meaning I find

rising from the ditch we walked by
daily for a week. We walked until

we outdistanced remarks, jumbled
scenery, the very forms of air.

As we too will shade from flesh to earth,
our smell finally made entirely

of wind, of word—so do we saunter
now past roadside brambles where nothing stirs.

Our walk is a homeward circuit
never complete. We live in someone

else's building, where other people's
dust endures in window cracks,

heating ducts, electric sockets
painted over. Smells we never

can place rise from the bathtub daily.
Memory like dust never dies

and never stops circulating: we live
with Santorio's dust, dinosaur bones,

pollen breathed by the Pharaohs,
each shooting star adding the sift

of space itself to our simmering.
Why shouldn't we be consoled

in our dying? I think of
the textbook woman, dead for decades,

whose cancer cells live on in labs
worldwide, their mad self-breeding fed

by the flat hand of science. Those cells
are not her, but now she is theirs,

their mindless generation her smell.
The woman I love does not die

except in my dreams, where I practice
taking what comfort I can in dust.

7.
I dreamed we stood by the edge
of a drained pond, which stank and shimmered

by moonlight. We could pick out
the ragged tracks of absent turtles.

A few fetid pools seethed with carp.
Two ducks circled overhead, speaking

in tongues. Hubcaps, snow tires, soda cans,
waterlogged sticks strewn everywhere,

everything glistening like what it was not,
and we found at last the words

to say so. The mud has a father,
we said, and the rain will replenish our joy.

8.
When the doctor said *malignant*
he also said *benign*, listing

a dozen earnest options, but
what we saw was dust furious

in sunlight, the cloud of our
unknowing as it darkened and swirled

its funnel cloud right down the street
we thought we knew, and I watched

her face pale as stormlight gathering.
Later we reckoned the odds, comfort

in its thousand homey nooks,
like the legends that survive each

tornado—how any house may lie
untouched next to the kindling

and smoke next door, how a cat may trot
unharmed from the black sky and land

home on her own roof, too stunned
to scratch the man who retrieves her.

If we were small enough we'd feel
fire and flood and earthquake that storm

through the cells daily. We'd know
the dust cloud of the ordinary,

where mites tinier than grains of sand
live on our random droppings—

flakes of skin settled to the rug,
pillow, upholstery—and thrive

for generations in the vacuum cleaner
with its blind and sudden wind,

where that burning smell is nothing
burning—just "resident dust,"

the nothing we see when drapes open,
motes in the light calling to mind

fall's antic swirl of leaves in wind,
settling nothing, being settled

at last in huge, temporary beds.
Does her tumor fatten on itself

in the dark in a wind like selfhood
enduring? Nothing is settled,

but as some dust never returns
to earth, just wavers and dances

so fine and dry it rises even
in the rain, let us breathe it in

and out until at worst we too will burn
with cool fire as the sun descends.